Seasons of a Beating Heart

Seasons of a Beating Heart

a poetry collection

Justine Marie Biondi

gatekeeper press
Columbus, Ohio

SEASONS OF A BEATING HEART

Published by Gatekeeper Press
2167 Stringtown Rd, Suite 109
Columbus, OH 43123-2989
www.GatekeeperPress.com

Library of Congress Control Number: 2022934035

ISBN (paperback): 9781662926341
eISBN: 9781662926358

To Vanessa,

Like lavender fields
Your presence is infinite
Vast as nature's will

You are so deeply missed.

Contents

Author's Note

Our life journey mirrors nature in many ways, especially the changing of the seasons. We can learn so much from nature by relating her constant ebb and flow to our own lives. Many of these poems draw inspiration from nature and the ever-changing world around us. I find comfort in knowing that we are not meant to remain stagnant. Like nature, the human experience is rooted in constant change and growth.

I have written this poetry collection over the past eight years, spanning from my teenage years into early adulthood. Writing poetry has allowed me to better cope with my emotions by understanding them through a different lens. These poems cover a wide range of life experiences including romantic, familial and platonic relationships, mental health, grief, self-love and growth.

This collection is organized into four chapters: Summer, Autumn, Winter and Spring. Each one portrays a different season of the heart. I encourage you to read the poems in any order you choose and to interpret them as you please. Whether you are experiencing summer, in love and grateful for the magic around you, or you are experiencing fall, heartbroken and uncertain about the future, I hope there are words in each chapter that help you feel seen, heard and understood. Though each of our journeys vary greatly, we are more alike than we may think. We will all experience love, loss, happiness and heartbreak. We all feel the effects of the changing of the seasons; but like nature, we will always bloom again.

Summer

Love and Wonder

Dusk

Layer upon layer
Of dusk-laden mountaintops,
A crisp breeze waves through my hair
Greeting my skin with risen bumps
And my eyes a watercolor sky.
It's not a chill that I feel,
But a comforting presence
From the life within the landscape
Painted in front of me.

Birds singing melodies high and low,
Leaves rustling neither fast nor slow.
A connected circle accompanies me
As I sit awestruck on crumpled weeds.

I gaze out into the world,
One little corner of the world
Where layer upon layer,
Dusk bathes the mountaintops,
And I wonder
Where this all began.

Sunlight

Your love is like sunlight,
Drenching flowers in full bloom.
A piece of home I always dreamt,
Blue skies at solar noon.

I found a home within myself,
Quite some time ago.
I looked around, nestled in,
And gave my roots room to grow.

I lived and loved there comfortably,
So when your sunlight broke through
And drenched my petals so effortlessly,
I knew I had found a home in you too.

Tender

Love is tender,
Like a beating heart
Without a cage.

Hand-Painted

Your eyes glisten beneath the moonlight,
Igniting a fire in my heart.
I press myself into your chest,
Living, breathing art.

You were painted by the same hand
That colors the skies above.
Both crafted on blank canvas,
Displayed in mind with love.

The more I gaze, the more I see
How beauty exists in harmony.

The magic held within the sky
Is the same magic found
Glistening in your eyes.

Colors of the Wind

You are the sun
Warming my veins
Sparking my heart.

You are the moon
Calming my soul
Together, apart.

You are the tide
Pulling me in
With magnetic roar.

You are the wind
Painting colors within
Spectrums never seen before.

Fairy Dust

I crave your touch like fairy dust.
A little sprinkle is all I need,
But I would bathe in it if I could
To feel alive and whimsically free.

Magic happens when we touch,
When I fall into your embrace.
My body melts into a sea of you,
Then vanishes without a trace.

I always dreamt of touching fairy dust,
Dancing beneath it like falling rain.
Now my dreams live and breathe
Lying with you, wide awake.

Photographing the Moon

Have you ever tried photographing the moon?
Muted light, blurred edges,
A speckle in the nighttime sky.
Photos struggle to encompass
The moon's effervescent essence.
Natural beauty roots far deeper
Than what cameras may catch on film.

You, too, are the moon,
Exquisite and absolutely astounding.

Togetherness

Your soft eyes meet mine
Breathing life into my heart
I find solace here

Magic

Wonder eclipses my mind
As a full moon ascends slowly
Over shadowed mountain ridges,
Casting a gracious golden glow
Onto indigo hues below.

Suddenly the world in front of me
Becomes a little too great
For my mind to grasp,
Like holding on to waves
Or grabbing on to wind.

Impossible.

If I had ever lost sight of life's magic,
I certainly found it tonight.

Selfless Love

As the sun sleeps,
She casts her light
Onto the moon's darkened face,
So that she too
Can light up the sky.

Beating

I move your palm gently
And place it over your heart.

Do you feel that beating?
You are living art.
Please be kind to yourself
In every way you can.
We're all trying our best
To be human.
That's all we can ask
Of ourselves in this life,
So please be patient
And indulge in your light.
You deserve the world
With warm love abound.
Please be kind to yourself
From the inside out.

Open Flame

Love is an open flame—
Some flicker atop a candle,
Others consume a forest.

What Loving You is Like

It's a perfect intertwining of two woven hands.
It's an anchor plunging into bottomless sand.
It's an untouched bullseye impaled by a dart.
It's a butterfly fluttering deep in the heart.

It's an ocean unfolding an infinity of waves.
It's a warmness radiating off magnetic flames.
It's a shooting star blazing across backlit skies.
It's an energetic buzz from a natural high.

It's a mesmerization by the beauty of a soul.
It's replenishing of a heart that once had holes.
It's a light dancing around your effortless grace.
It's a feeling of home in your strong embrace.

Being in love with you is all things simple and all things
magnificent.

Beside the Fire

I found a home in you
Beside the fire
Burning within your heart.

On a cold winter's night,
You burn onto me
As I burn onto you.

My Guiding Light

As I meander down the cobblestones of life,
I take each step guided by your light,
Further illuminating the pathway ahead
Like reading a book, one I've never read.

You offer me warmth when nights grow cold,
Engulfed by wisdom and stories told.
You inspire me in ways no one can match,
Lending your hand and heart, forever attached.

I believe in myself enough to change tides,
To take colossal leaps and gentle strides.
Changing the world will come as we go,
But it is possible, and that I know.

You taught me strength among everything else,
To flourish within and believe in myself.
So now we meander down the cobblestones of life,
And we do it together guided by our light.

Sorbet Skies

Golden rays blanket your face,
Forging an orange glow.
Basking here in effortless grace,
Watching the colors grow.

Warming air surrounds us
Almost as if to whisper,
"Let go and please trust,
As currents do a river."

Humble artistry,
Casting sorbet hues.
I melt into the sky
And then melt into you.

Sea Glass Tides

You are the breeze grazing the sea,
Breathing life, above and beneath.
Ever changing in the most beautiful light,
Emitting warmth amid darkened nights.

You are a poem yourself, you see,
Beauty woven ever so gently.
Like the harmonious changing of sea glass tides,
Or the delicate flow drifting through rhymes.

I thank the stars for overlapping our lines,
Pausing life for just a moment in time.
Moments spent laughing, weightless once more,
Childlike souls renewed, restored.

To be in your life
Is to be in your light
And oh, what a special place to be.

Living Art

I see your magic.
I hope you do too.
No one else is painted
Exactly like you.

Orange Glow

I find myself tracing
The outline of your face,
From the bridge of your nose
To the delicate point of your chin.
I want to remember
How your skin feels
Against mine.
Like frostbitten hands
Warming up
Beside a fire's blaze.
You shield my body
With your orange glow,
Protecting my heart
From wind and snow.
You are the fire I seek
When the world freezes over.
You are the warmth that keeps me sane.
You are the fire in the dead of night—
Darkness interrupted
By your beautiful light.

True Love's Dance

"What do you miss most about him?"
I asked you after he passed.
"Dancing together, in his arms
Creating moments that will last.

The first thing I will do
When I see him once again
Is melt into his chest
And dance to no end.

When you venture on your own
And see two butterflies twirl,
Know my love and I are together,
Two souls in another world.

I know he is waiting patiently
For me on the other side
To resume our love's dance
And continue this beautiful ride."

If You Were to Leave Today

And if you were to leave today,
I promise I will find you
Somewhere along the way.

Our love has been made
And engraved in our hearts,
Ingrained in our souls,
Colored glimpses of art.

A love so deep
It transcends the ocean floor.
I cannot help thinking
We have met here before.

Two souls journeyed
From far across the way.
I dreamt of your love
Each and every day.

I like to believe
That this came from above.
From the angels watching,
Guiding us with love.

Somewhere amid creation and chaos,
Our cosmic love was born.
We are both made of stardust,
A true love to adorn.

So if you were to leave today,
I promise I will find you
Somewhere along the way.

Stardust transcends space,
Transcends time.
So does your love,
And so does mine.

I promise not to worry
When your time comes and goes.
I promise I will follow
Wherever you may go.

And if my time comes
Before it does yours,
Please know that our love
Reflects an open door.

It will forever remain open
For the tears and laughs we shared.
I promise you, my dear,
Our love won't go anywhere.

When our time comes
To reunite once more,
I promise to embrace you
Like we never have before.

Bathed in stardust,
Shining with our might,
Dancing under galaxies
Basking in our light.

Take my hand
As I take yours,
Stronger than before,
Together once more.

Night Owl

Night blankets my vision
As the moon rises from slumber.
Even as she sleeps,
She roars magnetic thunder.

I wonder what she dreams about
With gravity-laden eyes.
Does she dream of other galaxies
Or find comfort within our skies?

Perhaps she drifts back and forth
Between what could have been
And what is,
Keeping her up as her mind spins.

When night washes over
Like most of us, I suppose,
Wonder drifts through our thoughts
Of possibilities unknown.

And yet we are here,
And here for a reason.
Whatever we may find
With each passing season.

To Love and Be Loved

Love is powerful and abundant.
I believe that's why we're here—
To love bravely and fiercely
Without hesitation or fear.

Love holds the heart together.
Love breaks the heart in two.
Through it all, how beautiful it is
To love and be loved by you.

Autumn

Heartbreak and Uncertainty

Not Meant to Last

Vibrant leaves dance gently
In the warm evening breeze.
We used to dance like that too,
Swaying lightly with ease.
With you, my heart felt safe
Like how tides trust the moon.
But we were a chapter not a book,
A setting sun before noon.
I knew that some stories
Faded out with the tides.
I hoped it wouldn't happen
To your love and mine.
Yet, here I am, watching leaves dance
Thinking of how we did the same.
But I don't know you anymore,
And I think that's okay.
We were good for a while,
But we were not meant to last.
We were only a chapter,
Love bound to the past.

Gray Skies

Stormy seas,
Blurred horizons,
Nothing here is clear.
Ice cold droplets pelt my skin
Drenching me with fear.

I pray for the passing
Of the storm overhead,
As I pray for the light
To shine up ahead.

Just a little guidance
I need to persevere.
Rain down on me, please
As you rain down on me here.

Current

You are the current
Dragging me out to sea.
The more I try to fight it,
The further I am dragged.

Three Words

I can't even say it out loud
In a quiet room by myself,
Let alone say it out loud
Looking into your eyes.

I'm scared of your response
Because I know I won't hear it back.

There may come a time
When it slips past my lips
And falls onto yours.
But until then,
My heart is the only place
Those three words exist.

I just wish they didn't
Burn a hole in my chest.

Barren Love

I whisper your name,
Waiting for a sound,
But all I feel are chills,
With silence all around.
Maybe that's the sound
That I needed to hear.
Well, I hear it now,
From ear to ear.
The wind doesn't care
That it's blowing so cold,
For it wears a coat
Bearing lies that it told.
Bits of glass puncture my feet
Walking back and forth
On barren concrete.
I search for protection
To warm what remains,
But everything has holes
And is covered in stains.
I whisper your name,
Waiting for a sound,
But all I feel are chills
With silence all around.

Irony

When we first met,
You asked who hurt me
As I was so afraid
Of letting you in.

Then I let you in,
Only to be hurt
In the same way I tried
So hard to avoid.

Ironic, isn't it?

Bitter

Your name is bitter on my tongue.
I cringe as it escapes my lips.
I said goodbye to sweetness long ago.
We were always a sinking ship.

Repetition

I always find myself
Rereading the same chapter
Over
And over
And over again.
I've memorized the beginning and middle,
And I know how it ends.
The words are already written.
The ending is already made.
But still I reread it
Over
And over
And over again.
I wasn't sure why,
But I guess it's because
It's the only chapter in my book
That's written
About you.

Burning Bridges

I never believed in burning bridges,
But sometimes the best way to get across the river
Is to swim through it.
To swim through the ashes gathering on the surface.
To swim against the current,
And let it wash away the pain.
I never believed in burning bridges
Until I realized that the only way
To get across the river
Is by getting over you.

Friends Can Break You Too

Your words were daggers.
They destroyed me,
Bludgeoned me,
Left me cradling my stomach,
Praying for the pain to go away.
My stomach, my throat and my heart—
Each torn apart
From every single blow.
The dagger that you held
Ripped gashes so deeply in my soul
That they were big enough
For my blood
To spill out in pools.
And all I could do
Was bear witness
To my wounds.
But what's worst isn't the dagger,
Or the damage it caused,
But the fact that it was you
Who held the knife.
The person who I thought
Would be the one to save me from any pain
Was the one inflicting my wounds,
And I don't know how to stop the bleeding.

Unfinished Chapters

Closure doesn't always come
From the ones we need it from.
Not everyone you share your heart with
Will have the same heart as you.
Unfinished chapters are written into our story too,
But that doesn't mean we should stop reading,
For something better will come along soon.

2020

Heavy clouds drain themselves
As droplets pound the pavement.
My tears cascade too
Turning my body blue.
I forget how it feels
To breathe in deeply
And know everything will be okay.
Day after night,
Night after day,
We dance in circles
Waiting for better news,
For a fight we will not lose.
Each day shows higher numbers
And less hope
For a turnaround soon.
I wonder when life will return,
When life will resume.
I hope this rain nourishes our roots.
I hope this rain subsides soon
Some way, somehow,
Rather than drown us out
As it feels right now.

Waning and Waxing

Perhaps the moon wanes and waxes
In reflection of ourselves.
We cannot always shine
As brightly as our might allows.
Sometimes only a sliver of light
Holds enough power to break through.
That doesn't mean we aren't whole,
For even the moon needs rest too.

Thicker Than Water

I'm yelling into a void
Begging for you to understand
How many times you've hurt me.
I should be caressed by your hand.
Instead you hold me,
Fragile as humans are
And smash me into the floor.
It is rather bizarre.
I can't understand you
And the love you have for me
Because time and time again,
You toss me to the sea
Without thought,
Without apology.

My pleas remain unfelt, unheard,
Falling onto deaf ears, every word.

Emotional Exhaustion

Feeling numb
When all warmth evades,
Leaving me senseless
To my own self.
Engulfed by flames
Or waves,
Could be either.
I can't even tell.

Residual Smoke

Tears swell behind their eyes,
Steady and ferocious,
Like waves building gradually
Before crashing atop the surface.
I have watched these waves build
Time and time again
And have watched them crash,
Over and over again,
Always wondering
When the crashing would end.

Both pairs of eyes
Are now clouded over
With their own misery.
My heart yearns for theirs
To flutter once more,
Even if they flutter with someone else.
I know what love looks like;
Gravity tugs at my heartstrings
Knowing this is a raw example
Of what love is not.

Perhaps love resided here years ago,
Perhaps in a time before my own.

But we can all see clearly now
That the flames have been blown out.
As we sit here together in a darkened room
Watching the residual smoke drift out.

Fires

Fires burn deep within your heart,
Inciting fear and anguish,
Slowly tearing you apart.

You feed them
Like birds flying into a lion's den.

Consumed by blackened smoke, you shout,
"When will I stop fueling the fires?
When will I finally put them out?"

Shadows

I ponder the comfort you find
While hiding in your shadows.
Does solitude lead to loneliness,
Or does solitude lead to solace?

I try peering into the cave
In which you rest your head,
Only to find dense fog,
Gray clouds lingering up ahead.

I don't want to be here
Hidden away from light.
I want to dance blissfully
On a warm summer night.

You can keep your shadows,
Your fog and your cave.
I will go on elsewhere
Unbound and willingly unafraid.

Through the Dust

We cannot control why things happen,
But we can control how we adjust.
For life is an unwashed window—
To see outside, we must peer through the dust.

Winter

Grief and Loss

Waves

Grief is not a single wave
Crashing onto the sand
And never touched upon again.
It is a fluctuating string
Of ripples, waves and mavericks
Continuously folding and unfolding
Onto the shore
Until the shore, itself,
Eventually recedes back home.

Internal Rivers

Time passes by,
Staining my cheeks
With deepened rivers.

Forever
Never

These words haunt my memories
As I reminisce about you,
Wondering where you have gone.

Wherever it is,
I hope that it's beautiful.

The Hand of Death

I'm no stranger to you.
I really wish I was.
I know you like the back of my hand,
But the pain never rescinds.
You still rip my heart into pieces
And throw them on the floor,
Somehow worse
Than each time before.
I'm no stranger to you.
God, I wish I was.
How many times can the heart break?
At least I know it's from love.

Anticipatory Grief

Black ravens howl
Embedding bitter darkness
Hope washes away

Uneven Timelines

A budding heart melding onto mine,
He snatched you away too soon.
Darkened shadows not on your side,
Too many chilled afternoons.

I was not done yet,
And neither were you.
But he loves roulette,
And he plays to lose.

He fated your journey
Selfishly in the dark
By cutting your life short,
Breath extinguishing sparks.

He doesn't care.
He never does.
He thrives on leaving ties undone.

I want to snatch him by the throat
For snatching yours too soon.
We had so much room left to grow,
More stargazing under the moon.

Together, apart
And everything in between.
Now I cling onto memories.
I was only eighteen.

I wish I could hug you,
Share worldviews of art,
Talk to you, hear you
Like we were never apart.

Right now my dreams will suffice.
Please visit as often as you like.

Lingering

As time passes on,
Grief will linger,
Hiding in the brightest places,
Appearing in the darkest.
Tears will cascade
Sometimes overflowing your walls.

There will always be that heaviness
Found deep within the heart,
Tugging on your strings
And reminding you
Of whom you have lost.

Slowly, life goes on.

You will see them again.
It just hurts knowing
That it will not be
Until your end begins.

Hope's Early Winter

Winter's eve sends chills down Hope's spine
As she collects the fallen leaves.
Even her body warmth,
Radiating with flames,
Cannot prevent us from freezing.

Snow falls earlier this year,
Blanketing the soil in frost.
No longer do her footprints
Softly imprint dewy blades.
Instead the ground
Is now fluttered with ash.

Like a butterfly without its wings,
She has nowhere to fly.
We have become lost within the haze,
Tussled back and forth beneath the waves.
Taking steps neither forward nor back
As the world appears still,
Frozen in time
While moving at the speed of light.

She watches silently from afar
As the snow buries us all.
With her hand outstretched towards our own
She reminds us of clearer skies.
Beyond the distant horizon,
We will rise.

Inner Journey

I see your journey
Darkened from pain's deep slumber
I hope you still dream

When the World Won't Stop Spinning

How does the world keep spinning
Even after you are gone?
Doesn't it know you're not here?
Doesn't it know you've moved on?

Why won't the world stop spinning
Like my world has here?
I'm broken by your passing.
I'm scared you'll disappear.

I want to find you,
Wherever you have gone.
But the world won't stop spinning.
I feel so withdrawn.

I don't know this place
Without you here.
I miss your sweet face.
It's all so unclear.

I wish the world would stop spinning
So I can catch my breath.
I forgot how to breathe
Soon after your death.

Can you visit me, please,
In my dreams somehow?
The world won't stop spinning.
I need you right now.

Tell me it will be okay,
And that I will see you soon.
Maybe in the breeze
Or the shine of the moon.

How does the world keep spinning
Even after you are gone?
I don't understand
How to go on.

Blaring Silence

Silence blares in the wake of your absence,
Like sirens signaling for attention to be paid
To the stillness of rooms once filled with your laugh,
To the emptiness of halls once warmed by your steps.
Who knew silence could be so loud?
It's all I hear now.
I wish so badly to hear you instead.

Broken Promises

How much promise we hold
When we enter this world.
How solemnly our hearts fold
When promises break too soon.
Unspent time,
Unhealed wounds.
Broken without reason
In the coldest season.
Where is such promise now?

Perhaps within those moments
Lived by you
And shared with your light.
You were the promise
In the dead of night.
Here, you will continue
Through the hearts of many.
I promise to hold you
Forever and plenty.

Checking In

It's been a while since I've seen you.
When was the last time you checked in?
I hope you do often,
Peering outside from within.
Have you seen who I've become?
How much I've grown up?
I wish you were here.
There's so much to fill you in on.
I'm older now, quite wiser too.
I wish you were here.
Our conversations are overdue.
There's so much I didn't say.
I was too young to understand
Who I was or where I was headed.
I wish you had been here along the way.
It's been a while since I've seen you.
When was the last time you checked in?
I still talk to you every day,
Hoping you hear the words I say.
I miss you and I love you
And so much more.
I hope you check in often,
Like you always did before.

Missing You

Memories unearth
Breaking my heart in two halves
Bleeding from absence

As Nature Feels the Wind

I envy the palms
Waving ferociously in the wind,
Overtaken by such natural force.
I wish you would do the same,
Wave ferociously through me
Unmistaken by your name.

I crave your presence,
Amid the cloud of your absence.
I crave feeling you as I had.
Your warm embrace,
Your contagious laugh,
Light on your beautiful face.

I envy the palms
As they sway back and forth,
Touched by nature's breath.
I wish you would do the same,
Wave through me as wind waves through trees,
Naturally and beautifully untamed.

Perhaps you already do.

Feathered Clouds

I see you in gently feathered clouds,
Highlighted fuchsia by the setting sun.
I see you in sparkling ocean waves,
Folding seamlessly one by one.
You still so easily caress my heart,
Even while being worlds apart.
For what would this life even mean
If your beauty was nowhere to be seen?
You were here, and here you will be
In all the beauty and magic surrounding me.

The Beauty of Grief

In the end,
A life without grief
Is a life without love,
And a life without love
Is not living at all.

My Rainbow

I'll miss our cuddles, your sweet kisses and love.
You were my precious friend sent from above.
Loyal in your heart, your beauty and soul.
Together with you, I never felt so whole.
You were my rainbow, hope after a storm.
With you, my heart was safe and warm.
I hope you are lighter now, free of pain.
I'll be sure to look for you after the rain.

Until we meet again
My beautiful friend.

Growing Pains

Our hearts grow through pain,
Through the holes left behind
That have been flooded by rain.

In time, the rain may cease just enough
For flowers to bloom
And fill those holes
With more beauty than pain.

In time, we may reminisce on the love
Still tethered so intimately to our hearts
And bathe in the warmth left behind.

Their absence will not hurt any less,
But growing gardens from their love
May bring comfort and peaceful rest.

As I Roam

You have never been so close,
But you have never seemed so far.
Once a soul here on earth,
Now a soul in my heart.

I will love you forever
And bring you with me as I roam.
In my mind and my heart,
You will always have a home.

Poppy

What began as a seed
Blossomed into a flower.
Strong, wise and beautiful,
It was practically perfect.

One day the winds picked up,
And rain soon followed.

Not all things beautiful last forever.

But with every gust of wind,
Every glimmer of sun,
And every drop of rain,
The poppy's memory lives on.

Everything the flower ever graced
Now shares its beauty with the world.
The poppy may have withered,
But its spirit will never die.

Forever, its soul lives around us.
Forever, its love lives within us.

Cashmere Sweaters

Your cashmere sweaters still hang
Silently in your closet,
Like a time capsule
From life's most beautiful days.
I can still picture you wearing them
On chilly autumn afternoons.
The amber sun striking your face,
Your perfect profile lightly traced.

It's been a while since I've hugged you,
So I hug your sweaters instead,
Breathing in traces of your scent,
Imagining what my world would be like
If you were still here in it.

My days have molded around your absence.
I still need reminders that you were here,
So I open your capsuled closet
And use your sweaters for my tears.
They remind me that you existed,
And you weren't just a beautiful dream
That I forged in my mind
From all the beauty that could be.

I picture you wearing these sweaters
While holding me right here,
Rather than me clinging desperately
On to your worn cashmere.

Stained Glass

Broken and shattered
Sunlight peeks through jagged glass
It shines once again

Spring

Growth and Self-Love

Change Can Be Good Too

Do leaves fear change as they turn from green to brown?
Or do they admire their changing colors under the autumn sun?
Do they fear their breakage amid winter's hold,
Or do they understand how nature unfolds?
The leaves will fall and grow back one day.
Growth follows change in a beautiful way.
I know winter doesn't last forever,
And that spring will follow soon.
I shouldn't fear change.
I know nature will bloom.
She always does.
Change can be good too.

Dove in Morning Gray

I saw a dove outside my window
As I got ready for the day.
She perched herself on a barren tree
In the mist of morning gray.
She stayed there for a while,
Bringing warmth to the gloom.
I couldn't help but wonder,
Does she know of me too?
Is this a friend of mine
Who waved her hand long ago?
Life is better with hope,
Like finding grass beneath snow.
She fluffed her feathers
And sang her song
Then she flew away,
My eyes trailing along.
You brightened my days,
Like this dove did today.
So I'm embracing its presence
As if it were you.
Please visit again soon.

Nature's Resilience

Let us never forget nature's resilience,
And her cyclical commitment
To change, rebirth and growth.
Let us never forget our own resilience,
As we are nature in the flesh.
We are the same breath of wind
That rustles red oak leaves.
We are the same beam of light
That feeds flowers and trees.
The seasons change as we grow,
For our beating hearts ebb and flow.
Let us never forget nature's resilience.
Let us never forget our own.

Steady Hands

I fell in love rather quickly,
Pouring my fluid heart
Into someone else's glass,
As they poured theirs into mine.
Neither have overflown,
Only expanded with time.

Falling in love with myself
Has taken slower strides.
Pouring my heart into my own glass
Is like swimming through riptides,
Constantly spilling,
Always pushing myself aside.

I struggle to move with steady hands.
I struggle to keep my glass filled where I stand.

But just as my heart
Fills someone else's glass,
Someday my heart will fill mine too.
And it will be filled to the brim,
Steady, as I move.

I am learning how to love myself
In the same way I know
How to love someone else.

Riding the Waves

Ferocious and gentle as morning rain,
The tides will wane, the pain will fade.
Ripples, waves and all movement in between,
The swells will eventually cease, you see.
Even if just for a moment, to center and breathe.

Just ride the waves a little bit longer.
We are much stronger than we believe.

Jupiter's Orbit

I saw Jupiter last night smiling at me from above.
I gazed at her with wonder, with a curious love.
She hasn't traveled this way in quite some time.
Has she finally found herself in the winter sky?

She's enchanting, like raindrops in a drought.
For too long, her light has been burnt out.
She has broken the chains holding her down.
The power within herself has been found.

She can move mountains, she could all along.
She just couldn't figure out where she belonged.
Maybe with others, with planets far away?
Right here, her own orbit, is where she should stay.

I saw Jupiter last night smiling at me from above.
I saw her shining, wrapped up in love.
Love from herself, then love from others.
She lights up the sky in glorious colors.

Wherever she goes, she's in good hands,
Trusting herself on where she will land.

The Most Valuable Friendship

Once I learned the value
Of being my own best friend,
Everything started falling into place.

Midnight Stars

These midnight stars shine so brightly,
Gently flooding my room with light.
When I have no candles left to burn,
I can always count on them at night
To burn on my behalf too
And show me wondrous places
My eyes have yet to view.

These midnight stars allow me to rest
And recharge my own light,
So I can burn enough for us all,
Come tomorrow's midnight.
I really hope these stars know
How much I appreciate their glow,
Especially on nights when I feel alone.

They always shine so brightly,
Even within the darkest of skies.
I can't say the same for myself,
But just know that I try.
Whenever I borrow
Just a speckle of their light,
I know my tomorrow will be alright.

I don't think they mind
Sharing their light with me too,
And if they do,
I'll return the favor soon.
After all, I am a midnight star too.
The only difference being I shine on land,
And they shine beside the moon.

Following the Wind

You ask me where I'm headed,
As if seeds know where they'll land.
I float along with the breeze
Above valleys and mountains.

Life appears more colorful
With my head out of the sand.
So when you ask me where I'm headed,
Trusting the wind is my plan.

Floating freely,
Blissfully in the breeze,
Enjoying my journey
Wherever it may take me.

Still As Nature

I take comfort in knowing
We are as still as nature,
Being still, not at all.

It's okay to run.
It's okay to stall.
It's okay to climb.
It's okay to fall.

There is no destination,
Only growth as we age.
Blooming into ourselves
With each passing day.

Rebloom

As winter burns brightly,
Nature sheds her leaves,
Burdened, broken and bare
By frosted tips
And weakened grips.
The trees will rebloom
When warming air restores,
And they will emerge
Stronger than before.

You will too.

Wanderer

She wanders after dusk
Deeply into the forest,
Uncovering new sounds,
Breaking new grounds.
She treks on
Delving deeper into darkness,
Confronting her doubts.
The noises do not shake her,
For she is bathed in love
And guided by moonlight.

Mirror

When I gaze into the mirror
Looking deeply into my eyes,
Hundreds of thoughts flood my mind,
Recollecting years of time.

Am I making my younger self proud?
Does she like who I've become?
She used to view life with wonder
Before the world made her numb.

She lived each day simply,
Finding magic in every cloud.
She danced beneath the sun.
I only want to make her proud.

When I gaze into the mirror
Looking deeply into my eyes,
I still see that little girl.
She has never left my side.

For her, I will seek magic
Within every tree and ocean wave.
For we have built this home together,
And I would like for her to stay.

Rebirth

As winter becomes spring,
A sparrow awakens.
She glides through warming air,
Uplifted by the sun's embrace.
No longer inhibited by winter's chill,
The sparrow spreads her wings,
Dancing freely through open skies.
She never feared freedom,
But with this new dawn,
She soars without limits.

Little Things

It's the little things in life,
The little things to treasure.
For when you focus on the good,
The good becomes better.

Life is easier this way.
Breathing becomes lighter.
When grateful for the little things,
Hope burns a little brighter.

Connected Beings

I gaze upon the sparkling river,
Glistening from the first beams of May.
A white swan swims upstream
Delicately paving her way.

She sails ahead confidently,
Without pause or trepidation.
Venturing alone on rippled waters,
Toward a newfound destination.

I wonder where she is headed.
I wonder if she even knows.
She swims around the riverbend.
My eyes follow as she goes.

She soon disappears from sight,
Like white clouds bathed in sunlight.
Her journey is special like yours and mine.
Paths overlapped for a moment in time.

She is a stranger to me,
While a friend to others.
But who are we, really,
If not one with each other?

We are all connected
Like the roots of elder trees.
Filled with love and admiration
Is how we should always be.

Flowers Always Bloom

Better days are coming.
Trust in the tides.
Flowers always bloom,
And they bloom in strides.

Inner Strength

By grace, she glimmers
Like a beam of light,
Striking through withered oak
In the dead of night.

She lights up the world,
Roots growing at her feet.
She leads with courage
And a tender heartbeat.

Desert Rain

I thought there was strength
In sacrificing my needs for others,
But it's quite the opposite.
Over time, the light that once burned
So brightly within myself
Has slowly faded
Into all but the smallest ember—
Still burning, but barely there.
I tried so hard to brighten the lights around me
That I had no light left
To brighten my own.
My cup, once filled to the brim,
Has depleted completely,
Leaving me curled over
In an empty, dimly lit space,
Barely big enough for myself
To exist.

All this time, I thought I acted out of love,
And maybe I did;
But all that energy I poured
So willingly into other people
Has left me barren, like a desert
That hasn't felt rain in years.
I forgive myself for not pouring energy
Into myself as eagerly as I did for others.
I forgive myself for taking a little too long to realize
That I was hurting myself
In an attempt to ease everyone else's pain.
But I see it now.

I see the light after losing sight of my own.
I'm sorry I haven't looked after myself
As tenderly as I needed to.
But I'm here now,
And I'm never leaving again.

Gardens

Daisies don't compare themselves
To roses planted nearby.
They don't sit and worry,
"Am I blooming on time?
Are my petals too white?
Should my leaves have more shine?"
Instead they bask in the sun
And let nature handle the rest,
Knowing they are perfect as they come,
Never to consider or second guess
The color of their petals
Or the shine of their leaves.
They thrive as they are
And bloom as they please.
Gardens are most beautiful
When different flowers grow.
If every flower was a rose,
Red is all we would know.

The Sun's Beginning

How did the sun emerge?
From being born of fire
Or reaping its own skies?
No matter the source
The sun emerged still,
And it glistens with diamonds.

Perfectly Imperfect

Humans are not meant to be perfect.
We are designed with imperfections,
Carefully and intentionally.
So why do we chase this concept of perfection
When it doesn't even exist,
And can never be attained?
We created this concept
At the hands of our youth.
Comparing ourselves
Until we become dust in the wind.
Until we have lost sight
Of the things that make us whole.
We are beautiful because we are imperfect.
Our scars, cracks, holes and irregular lines
This is where our beauty shines.
So who are we to dim our own light
On the basis of being perfect?
When being imperfect
Is exactly what we are supposed to be.

Rise

As the sun sets,
So do we.
As the sun rises,
So will we.

We will not be the same,
But we will always rise again,
Ascending higher
Than we ever had before.

Enough

I feel like I'm not doing enough
To make ends meet
Between my hands and my heart.
Maybe I am,
Maybe I'm not.

I feel constant pressure within myself
Like a rubber band
Stretching further and further apart
Every day
Until one day
It breaks
By the same two hands
That wished to keep it whole.

I don't want to reach that day
When my walls become so weak
That they crumble away.

So I must push down this feeling
Of inadequacy
And embrace the day-to-day
Struggle,
Triumph,
And everything in between.
As long as I lead with love
And a mind filled with hope,
Then I know I am doing enough.

Morning Sun

Icicles form on my windowsill,
Hanging in dawn's early age.
They are delicately pointed
Like ballerinas on stage.

As the morning sun rises
Over chilled barren trees,
The icicles begin to melt,
Dripping in the breeze.

How quickly they form,
How quickly they soften.
Much like our thoughts,
Changing swiftly often.

Sometimes all we need
Is a little morning sun,
And then we can breathe,
And then we can run.

Phoenix

And through it all,
Here we stand
On top of boulders
That once anchored us
So deeply into sand.
Like a phoenix rising from its ashes
Again and again.

And through it all,
Here we stand
With scars as deep, complex and beautiful
As Arizona canyons at dawn.
Here we stand on top of our pain,
Rising above it all
Again and again.

Resilient to our core,
Human evermore.

CPSIA information can be obtained
at www.ICGtesting.com
Printed in the USA
JSHW071200160423
40296JS00004B/13